THIS BOOK BELONGS TO:

_____

GARDEN LAYOUT

GARDEN LAYOUT

PLANT LOG

PLANT NAME

CROP TYPE

Plant Type	Sun Requirement	Water Requirement	Life Cycle
○ Vegetable			○ Annual
○ Fruit			○ Biennial
○ Herb			○ Perennial
○ Ornamental			

SOWN FROM SEED

Supplier

Cost

Date Sown

Date Germinated

Date Planted Out

Date Harvested/Bloomed

STARTED TRANSPLANT

Supplier

Cost

Date Planted

Date Harvested/Bloomed

GROWING NOTES (pests, fertilizers, disease, unexpected weather conditions, etc.)

OUTCOME

Total Yield in Pounds	Rate It?	Grow Again?
	① ② ③ ④ ⑤	YES // NO

PLANT LOG

PLANT NAME

CROP TYPE

Plant Type
O Vegetable
O Fruit
O Herb
O Ornamental

Sun Requirement

Water Requirement

Life Cycle
O Annual
O Biennial
O Perennial

SOWN FROM SEED

Supplier

Cost

Date Sown

Date Germinated

Date Planted Out

Date Harvested/Bloomed

STARTED TRANSPLANT

Supplier

Cost

Date Planted

Date Harvested/Bloomed

GROWING NOTES *(pests, fertilizers, disease, unexpected weather conditions, etc.)*

OUTCOME

Total Yield in Pounds

Rate It?
1 2 3 4 5

Grow Again?
YES // NO

PLANT LOG

> **PLANT NAME**

> **CROP TYPE**

Plant Type
- ○ Vegetable
- ○ Fruit
- ○ Herb
- ○ Ornamental

Sun Requirement

Water Requirement

Life Cycle
- ○ Annual
- ○ Biennial
- ○ Perennial

SOWN FROM SEED

Supplier

Cost

Date Sown

Date Germinated

Date Planted Out

Date Harvested/Bloomed

STARTED TRANSPLANT

Supplier

Cost

Date Planted

Date Harvested/Bloomed

GROWING NOTES *(pests, fertilizers, disease, unexpected weather conditions, etc.)*

OUTCOME

Total Yield in Pounds

Rate It?

1 2 3 4 5

Grow Again?

YES // NO

PLANT LOG

PLANT NAME

CROP TYPE

Plant Type
O Vegetable
O Fruit
O Herb
O Ornamental

Sun Requirement

Water Requirement

Life Cycle
○ Annual
○ Biennial
○ Perennial

SOWN FROM SEED

Supplier

Cost

Date Sown

Date Germinated

Date Planted Out

Date Harvested/Bloomed

STARTED TRANSPLANT

Supplier

Cost

Date Planted

Date Harvested/Bloomed

GROWING NOTES *(pests, fertilizers, disease, unexpected weather conditions, etc.)*

OUTCOME

Total Yield in Pounds

Rate It?

1 2 3 4 5

Grow Again?

YES // NO

PLANT LOG

PLANT NAME

CROP TYPE

Plant Type
O Vegetable
O Fruit
O Herb
O Ornamental

Sun Requirement

Water Requirement

Life Cycle
○ Annual
○ Biennial
○ Perennial

SOWN FROM SEED

Supplier

Cost

Date Sown

Date Germinated

Date Planted Out

Date Harvested/Bloomed

STARTED TRANSPLANT

Supplier

Cost

Date Planted

Date Harvested/Bloomed

GROWING NOTES (pests, fertilizers, disease, unexpected weather conditions, etc.)

OUTCOME

Total Yield in Pounds

Rate It?

Grow Again?

YES // NO

PLANT LOG

PLANT NAME

CROP TYPE

Plant Type	Sun Requirement	Water Requirement	Life Cycle
O Vegetable			O Annual
O Fruit			O Biennial
O Herb			O Perennial
O Ornamental			

SOWN FROM SEED

Supplier

Cost

Date Sown

Date Germinated

Date Planted Out

Date Harvested/Bloomed

STARTED TRANSPLANT

Supplier

Cost

Date Planted

Date Harvested/Bloomed

GROWING NOTES (pests, fertilizers, disease, unexpected weather conditions, etc.)

OUTCOME

Total Yield in Pounds

Rate It?

1 2 3 4 5

Grow Again?

YES // NO

PLANT LOG

> **PLANT NAME**

> **CROP TYPE**

Plant Type	Sun Requirement	Water Requirement	Life Cycle
○ Vegetable ○ Fruit ○ Herb ○ Ornamental			○ Annual ○ Biennial ○ Perennial

SOWN FROM SEED

Supplier   Cost

Date Sown

Date Germinated   Date Planted Out

Date Harvested/Bloomed

STARTED TRANSPLANT

Supplier

Cost

Date Planted

Date Harvested/Bloomed

GROWING NOTES *(pests, fertilizers, disease, unexpected weather conditions, etc.)*

OUTCOME

Total Yield in Pounds   Rate It?

1 2 3 4 5

Grow Again?

YES // NO

🌿 PLANT LOG 🌿

PLANT NAME

CROP TYPE

Plant Type
O Vegetable
O Fruit
O Herb
O Ornamental

Sun Requirement

Water Requirement

Life Cycle
O Annual
O Biennial
O Perennial

SOWN FROM SEED

Supplier

Cost

Date Sown

Date Germinated

Date Planted Out

Date Harvested/Bloomed

STARTED TRANSPLANT

Supplier

Cost

Date Planted

Date Harvested/Bloomed

GROWING NOTES (pests, fertilizers, disease, unexpected weather conditions, etc.)

OUTCOME

Total Yield in Pounds

Rate It?
1 2 3 4 5

Grow Again?
YES // NO

 # PLANT LOG

PLANT NAME

CROP TYPE

Plant Type	Sun Requirement	Water Requirement	Life Cycle
○ Vegetable			○ Annual
○ Fruit			○ Biennial
○ Herb			○ Perennial
○ Ornamental			

SOWN FROM SEED

Supplier

Cost

Date Sown

Date Germinated

Date Planted Out

Date Harvested/Bloomed

STARTED TRANSPLANT

Supplier

Cost

Date Planted

Date Harvested/Bloomed

GROWING NOTES *(pests, fertilizers, disease, unexpected weather conditions, etc.)*

OUTCOME

Total Yield in Pounds

Rate It?

1 2 3 4 5

Grow Again?

YES // NO

PLANT LOG

PLANT NAME

CROP TYPE

Plant Type
O Vegetable
O Fruit
O Herb
O Ornamental

Sun Requirement

Water Requirement

Life Cycle
○ Annual
○ Biennial
○ Perennial

SOWN FROM SEED

Supplier

Cost

Date Sown

Date Germinated

Date Planted Out

Date Harvested/Bloomed

STARTED TRANSPLANT

Supplier

Cost

Date Planted

Date Harvested/Bloomed

GROWING NOTES *(pests, fertilizers, disease, unexpected weather conditions, etc.)*

OUTCOME

Total Yield in Pounds

Rate It?

Grow Again?

YES // NO

PLANT LOG

PLANT NAME

CROP TYPE

Plant Type
O Vegetable
O Fruit
O Herb
O Ornamental

Sun Requirement

Water Requirement

Life Cycle
○ Annual
○ Biennial
○ Perennial

SOWN FROM SEED

Supplier

Cost

Date Sown

Date Germinated

Date Planted Out

Date Harvested/Bloomed

STARTED TRANSPLANT

Supplier

Cost

Date Planted

Date Harvested/Bloomed

GROWING NOTES *(pests, fertilizers, disease, unexpected weather conditions, etc.)*

OUTCOME

Total Yield in Pounds

Rate It?

Grow Again?

YES // NO

PLANT LOG

PLANT NAME

CROP TYPE

Plant Type
O Vegetable
O Fruit
O Herb
O Ornamental

Sun Requirement

Water Requirement

Life Cycle
O Annual
O Biennial
O Perennial

SOWN FROM SEED

Supplier

Cost

Date Sown

Date Germinated

Date Planted Out

Date Harvested/Bloomed

STARTED TRANSPLANT

Supplier

Cost

Date Planted

Date Harvested/Bloomed

GROWING NOTES *(pests, fertilizers, disease, unexpected weather conditions, etc.)*

OUTCOME

Total Yield in Pounds

Rate It?

Grow Again?

YES // NO

PLANT LOG

PLANT NAME

CROP TYPE

Plant Type
- O Vegetable
- O Fruit
- O Herb
- O Ornamental

Sun Requirement

Water Requirement

Life Cycle
- O Annual
- O Biennial
- O Perennial

SOWN FROM SEED

Supplier

Cost

Date Sown

Date Germinated

Date Planted Out

Date Harvested/Bloomed

STARTED TRANSPLANT

Supplier

Cost

Date Planted

Date Harvested/Bloomed

GROWING NOTES *(pests, fertilizers, disease, unexpected weather conditions, etc.)*

OUTCOME

Total Yield in Pounds

Rate It?

1 2 3 4 5

Grow Again?

YES // NO

PLANT LOG

PLANT NAME

CROP TYPE

Plant Type
O Vegetable
O Fruit
O Herb
O Ornamental

Sun Requirement

Water Requirement

Life Cycle
O Annual
O Biennial
O Perennial

SOWN FROM SEED

Supplier

Cost

Date Sown

Date Germinated

Date Planted Out

Date Harvested/Bloomed

STARTED TRANSPLANT

Supplier

Cost

Date Planted

Date Harvested/Bloomed

GROWING NOTES (pests, fertilizers, disease, unexpected weather conditions, etc.)

OUTCOME

Total Yield in Pounds

Rate It?

1 2 3 4 5

Grow Again?

YES // NO

PLANT LOG

PLANT NAME

CROP TYPE

Plant Type	Sun Requirement	Water Requirement	Life Cycle
◯ Vegetable			◯ Annual
◯ Fruit			◯ Biennial
◯ Herb			◯ Perennial
◯ Ornamental			

SOWN FROM SEED

Supplier

Cost

Date Sown

Date Germinated

Date Planted Out

Date Harvested/Bloomed

STARTED TRANSPLANT

Supplier

Cost

Date Planted

Date Harvested/Bloomed

GROWING NOTES *(pests, fertilizers, disease, unexpected weather conditions, etc.)*

OUTCOME

Total Yield in Pounds	Rate It?	Grow Again?
	① ② ③ ④ ⑤	YES // NO

PLANT LOG

PLANT NAME

CROP TYPE

Plant Type	Sun Requirement	Water Requirement	Life Cycle
O Vegetable O Fruit O Herb O Ornamental			O Annual O Biennial O Perennial

SOWN FROM SEED

Supplier

Cost

Date Sown

Date Germinated

Date Planted Out

Date Harvested/Bloomed

STARTED TRANSPLANT

Supplier

Cost

Date Planted

Date Harvested/Bloomed

GROWING NOTES *(pests, fertilizers, disease, unexpected weather conditions, etc.)*

OUTCOME

Total Yield in Pounds

Rate It?

Grow Again?

YES // NO

PLANT LOG

PLANT NAME

CROP TYPE

Plant Type	Sun Requirement	Water Requirement	Life Cycle
O Vegetable O Fruit O Herb O Ornamental			O Annual O Biennial O Perennial

SOWN FROM SEED

Supplier

Cost

Date Sown

Date Germinated

Date Planted Out

Date Harvested/Bloomed

STARTED TRANSPLANT

Supplier

Cost

Date Planted

Date Harvested/Bloomed

GROWING NOTES *(pests, fertilizers, disease, unexpected weather conditions, etc.)*

OUTCOME

Total Yield in Pounds

Rate It?

Grow Again?

YES // NO

PLANT LOG

PLANT NAME

CROP TYPE

Plant Type	Sun Requirement	Water Requirement	Life Cycle
O Vegetable O Fruit O Herb O Ornamental			O Annual O Biennial O Perennial

SOWN FROM SEED

Supplier

Cost

Date Sown

Date Germinated

Date Planted Out

Date Harvested/Bloomed

STARTED TRANSPLANT

Supplier

Cost

Date Planted

Date Harvested/Bloomed

GROWING NOTES *(pests, fertilizers, disease, unexpected weather conditions, etc.)*

OUTCOME

Total Yield in Pounds

Rate It?

Grow Again?

YES // NO

PLANT LOG

> **PLANT NAME**

> **CROP TYPE**

Plant Type
- ○ Vegetable
- ○ Fruit
- ○ Herb
- ○ Ornamental

Sun Requirement

Water Requirement

Life Cycle
- ○ Annual
- ○ Biennial
- ○ Perennial

SOWN FROM SEED

Supplier   Cost

Date Sown

Date Germinated   Date Planted Out

Date Harvested/Bloomed

STARTED TRANSPLANT

Supplier

Cost

Date Planted

Date Harvested/Bloomed

GROWING NOTES *(pests, fertilizers, disease, unexpected weather conditions, etc.)*

OUTCOME

Total Yield in Pounds

Rate It?

1 2 3 4 5

Grow Again?

YES // NO

PLANT LOG

PLANT NAME

CROP TYPE

Plant Type	Sun Requirement	Water Requirement	Life Cycle
O Vegetable			O Annual
O Fruit			O Biennial
O Herb			O Perennial
O Ornamental			

SOWN FROM SEED

Supplier

Cost

Date Sown

Date Germinated

Date Planted Out

Date Harvested/Bloomed

STARTED TRANSPLANT

Supplier

Cost

Date Planted

Date Harvested/Bloomed

GROWING NOTES *(pests, fertilizers, disease, unexpected weather conditions, etc.)*

OUTCOME

Total Yield in Pounds

Rate It?

Grow Again?

YES // NO

PLANT LOG

PLANT NAME

CROP TYPE

Plant Type
- O Vegetable
- O Fruit
- O Herb
- O Ornamental

Sun Requirement

Water Requirement

Life Cycle
- O Annual
- O Biennial
- O Perennial

SOWN FROM SEED

Supplier

Cost

Date Sown

Date Germinated

Date Planted Out

Date Harvested/Bloomed

STARTED TRANSPLANT

Supplier

Cost

Date Planted

Date Harvested/Bloomed

GROWING NOTES *(pests, fertilizers, disease, unexpected weather conditions, etc.)*

OUTCOME

Total Yield in Pounds

Rate It?

1 2 3 4 5

Grow Again?

YES // NO

PLANT LOG

PLANT NAME

CROP TYPE

Plant Type	Sun Requirement	Water Requirement	Life Cycle
O Vegetable O Fruit O Herb O Ornamental			O Annual O Biennial O Perennial

SOWN FROM SEED

Supplier   Cost

Date Sown

Date Germinated   Date Planted Out

Date Harvested/Bloomed

STARTED TRANSPLANT

Supplier

Cost

Date Planted

Date Harvested/Bloomed

GROWING NOTES *(pests, fertilizers, disease, unexpected weather conditions, etc.)*

OUTCOME

Total Yield in Pounds   Rate It?

Grow Again?

YES // NO

 # PLANT LOG

PLANT NAME

CROP TYPE

Plant Type

○ Vegetable
○ Fruit
○ Herb
○ Ornamental

Sun Requirement

Water Requirement

Life Cycle

○ Annual
○ Biennial
○ Perennial

SOWN FROM SEED

Supplier

Cost

Date Sown

Date Germinated

Date Planted Out

Date Harvested/Bloomed

STARTED TRANSPLANT

Supplier

Cost

Date Planted

Date Harvested/Bloomed

GROWING NOTES *(pests, fertilizers, disease, unexpected weather conditions, etc.)*

OUTCOME

Total Yield in Pounds

Rate It?

1 2 3 4 5

Grow Again?

YES // NO

🌿 PLANT LOG 🌿

PLANT NAME

CROP TYPE

Plant Type	Sun Requirement	Water Requirement	Life Cycle
O Vegetable			O Annual
O Fruit			O Biennial
O Herb			O Perennial
O Ornamental			

SOWN FROM SEED

Supplier

Cost

Date Sown

Date Germinated

Date Planted Out

Date Harvested/Bloomed

STARTED TRANSPLANT

Supplier

Cost

Date Planted

Date Harvested/Bloomed

GROWING NOTES *(pests, fertilizers, disease, unexpected weather conditions, etc.)*

OUTCOME

Total Yield in Pounds

Rate It?

1 2 3 4 5

Grow Again?

YES // NO

PLANT LOG

PLANT NAME

CROP TYPE

Plant Type	Sun Requirement	Water Requirement	Life Cycle
○ Vegetable			○ Annual
○ Fruit			○ Biennial
○ Herb			○ Perennial
○ Ornamental			

SOWN FROM SEED

Supplier   Cost

Date Sown

Date Germinated   Date Planted Out

Date Harvested/Bloomed

STARTED TRANSPLANT

Supplier

Cost

Date Planted

Date Harvested/Bloomed

GROWING NOTES *(pests, fertilizers, disease, unexpected weather conditions, etc.)*

OUTCOME

Total Yield in Pounds   Rate It?   Grow Again?

1 2 3 4 5   **YES // NO**

PLANT LOG

PLANT NAME

CROP TYPE

Plant Type
O Vegetable
O Fruit
O Herb
O Ornamental

Sun Requirement

Water Requirement

Life Cycle
O Annual
O Biennial
O Perennial

SOWN FROM SEED

Supplier

Cost

Date Sown

Date Germinated

Date Planted Out

Date Harvested/Bloomed

STARTED TRANSPLANT

Supplier

Cost

Date Planted

Date Harvested/Bloomed

GROWING NOTES *(pests, fertilizers, disease, unexpected weather conditions, etc.)*

OUTCOME

Total Yield in Pounds

Rate It?

Grow Again?

YES // NO

PLANT LOG

PLANT NAME

CROP TYPE

Plant Type
O Vegetable
O Fruit
O Herb
O Ornamental

Sun Requirement

Water Requirement

Life Cycle
O Annual
O Biennial
O Perennial

SOWN FROM SEED

Supplier

Cost

Date Sown

Date Germinated

Date Planted Out

Date Harvested/Bloomed

STARTED TRANSPLANT

Supplier

Cost

Date Planted

Date Harvested/Bloomed

GROWING NOTES *(pests, fertilizers, disease, unexpected weather conditions, etc.)*

OUTCOME

Total Yield in Pounds

Rate It?

1 2 3 4 5

Grow Again?

YES // NO

PLANT LOG

PLANT NAME

CROP TYPE

Plant Type	Sun Requirement	Water Requirement	Life Cycle
O Vegetable			O Annual
O Fruit			O Biennial
O Herb			O Perennial
O Ornamental			

SOWN FROM SEED

Supplier | Cost

Date Sown

Date Germinated | Date Planted Out

Date Harvested/Bloomed

STARTED TRANSPLANT

Supplier

Cost

Date Planted

Date Harvested/Bloomed

GROWING NOTES *(pests, fertilizers, disease, unexpected weather conditions, etc.)*

OUTCOME

Total Yield in Pounds | Rate It? | Grow Again?

1 2 3 4 5

YES // NO

PLANT LOG

PLANT NAME

CROP TYPE

Plant Type
- O Vegetable
- O Fruit
- O Herb
- O Ornamental

Sun Requirement

Water Requirement

Life Cycle
- O Annual
- O Biennial
- O Perennial

SOWN FROM SEED

Supplier

Cost

Date Sown

Date Germinated

Date Planted Out

Date Harvested/Bloomed

STARTED TRANSPLANT

Supplier

Cost

Date Planted

Date Harvested/Bloomed

GROWING NOTES *(pests, fertilizers, disease, unexpected weather conditions, etc.)*

OUTCOME

Total Yield in Pounds

Rate It?

1 2 3 4 5

Grow Again?

YES // NO

PLANT LOG

PLANT NAME

CROP TYPE

Plant Type	Sun Requirement	Water Requirement	Life Cycle
O Vegetable O Fruit O Herb O Ornamental			O Annual O Biennial O Perennial

SOWN FROM SEED

Supplier

Cost

Date Sown

Date Germinated

Date Planted Out

Date Harvested/Bloomed

STARTED TRANSPLANT

Supplier

Cost

Date Planted

Date Harvested/Bloomed

GROWING NOTES *(pests, fertilizers, disease, unexpected weather conditions, etc.)*

OUTCOME

Total Yield in Pounds

Rate It?

Grow Again?

YES // NO

PLANT LOG

PLANT NAME

CROP TYPE

Plant Type
-) Vegetable
-) Fruit
-) Herb
-) Ornamental

Sun Requirement

Water Requirement

Life Cycle
- ○ Annual
- ○ Biennial
- ○ Perennial

SOWN FROM SEED

Supplier

Cost

Date Sown

Date Germinated

Date Planted Out

Date Harvested/Bloomed

STARTED TRANSPLANT

Supplier

Cost

Date Planted

Date Harvested/Bloomed

GROWING NOTES *(pests, fertilizers, disease, unexpected weather conditions, etc.)*

OUTCOME

Total Yield in Pounds

Rate It?

1   2   3   4   5

Grow Again?

YES // NO

 # PLANT LOG

PLANT NAME

CROP TYPE

Plant Type	Sun Requirement	Water Requirement	Life Cycle
O Vegetable			O Annual
O Fruit			O Biennial
O Herb			O Perennial
O Ornamental			

SOWN FROM SEED

Supplier   Cost

Date Sown

Date Germinated   Date Planted Out

Date Harvested/Bloomed

STARTED TRANSPLANT

Supplier

Cost

Date Planted

Date Harvested/Bloomed

GROWING NOTES (pests, fertilizers, disease, unexpected weather conditions, etc.)

OUTCOME

Total Yield in Pounds	Rate It?	Grow Again?
		YES // NO

PLANT LOG

PLANT NAME

CROP TYPE

Plant Type
- O Vegetable
- O Fruit
- O Herb
- O Ornamental

Sun Requirement

Water Requirement

Life Cycle
- ○ Annual
- ○ Biennial
- ○ Perennial

SOWN FROM SEED

Supplier

Cost

Date Sown

Date Germinated   Date Planted Out

Date Harvested/Bloomed

STARTED TRANSPLANT

Supplier

Cost

Date Planted

Date Harvested/Bloomed

GROWING NOTES *(pests, fertilizers, disease, unexpected weather conditions, etc.)*

OUTCOME

Total Yield in Pounds

Rate It?

Grow Again?

YES // NO

PLANT LOG

PLANT NAME

CROP TYPE

Plant Type	Sun Requirement	Water Requirement	Life Cycle
O Vegetable O Fruit O Herb O Ornamental			O Annual O Biennial O Perennial

SOWN FROM SEED

Supplier

Cost

Date Sown

Date Germinated

Date Planted Out

Date Harvested/Bloomed

STARTED TRANSPLANT

Supplier

Cost

Date Planted

Date Harvested/Bloomed

GROWING NOTES *(pests, fertilizers, disease, unexpected weather conditions, etc.)*

OUTCOME

Total Yield in Pounds	Rate It?	Grow Again?
		**YES // NO**

PLANT LOG

PLANT NAME

CROP TYPE

Plant Type
- ◯ Vegetable
- ◯ Fruit
- ◯ Herb
- ◯ Ornamental

Sun Requirement

Water Requirement

Life Cycle
- ◯ Annual
- ◯ Biennial
- ◯ Perennial

SOWN FROM SEED

Supplier | Cost

Date Sown

Date Germinated | Date Planted Out

Date Harvested/Bloomed

STARTED TRANSPLANT

Supplier

Cost

Date Planted

Date Harvested/Bloomed

GROWING NOTES *(pests, fertilizers, disease, unexpected weather conditions, etc.)*

OUTCOME

Total Yield in Pounds | Rate It?

1 2 3 4 5

Grow Again?

YES // NO

PLANT LOG

PLANT NAME

CROP TYPE

Plant Type
O Vegetable
O Fruit
O Herb
O Ornamental

Sun Requirement

Water Requirement

Life Cycle
O Annual
O Biennial
O Perennial

SOWN FROM SEED

Supplier

Cost

Date Sown

Date Germinated

Date Planted Out

Date Harvested/Bloomed

STARTED TRANSPLANT

Supplier

Cost

Date Planted

Date Harvested/Bloomed

GROWING NOTES *(pests, fertilizers, disease, unexpected weather conditions, etc.)*

OUTCOME

Total Yield in Pounds

Rate It?

Grow Again?

YES // NO

PLANT LOG

PLANT NAME

CROP TYPE

Plant Type	Sun Requirement	Water Requirement	Life Cycle
) Vegetable) Fruit) Herb) Ornamental			○ Annual ○ Biennial ○ Perennial

SOWN FROM SEED

Supplier   Cost

Date Sown

Date Germinated   Date Planted Out

Date Harvested/Bloomed

STARTED TRANSPLANT

Supplier

Cost

Date Planted

Date Harvested/Bloomed

GROWING NOTES *(pests, fertilizers, disease, unexpected weather conditions, etc.)*

OUTCOME

Total Yield in Pounds	Rate It?	Grow Again?
	① ② ③ ④ ⑤	**YES // NO**

PLANT LOG

PLANT NAME

CROP TYPE

Plant Type
O Vegetable
O Fruit
O Herb
O Ornamental

Sun Requirement

Water Requirement

Life Cycle
○ Annual
○ Biennial
○ Perennial

SOWN FROM SEED

Supplier

Cost

Date Sown

Date Germinated

Date Planted Out

Date Harvested/Bloomed

STARTED TRANSPLANT

Supplier

Cost

Date Planted

Date Harvested/Bloomed

GROWING NOTES *(pests, fertilizers, disease, unexpected weather conditions, etc.)*

OUTCOME

Total Yield in Pounds

Rate It?

Grow Again?

YES // NO

🌿 PLANT LOG 🌿

PLANT NAME

CROP TYPE

Plant Type	Sun Requirement	Water Requirement	Life Cycle
O Vegetable O Fruit O Herb O Ornamental	☀️ 🌤️ ☁️	💧 💧 💧	O Annual O Biennial O Perennial

SOWN FROM SEED

Supplier   Cost

Date Sown

Date Germinated   Date Planted Out

Date Harvested/Bloomed

STARTED TRANSPLANT

Supplier

Cost

Date Planted

Date Harvested/Bloomed

GROWING NOTES *(pests, fertilizers, disease, unexpected weather conditions, etc.)*

OUTCOME

Total Yield in Pounds | Rate It?

1 2 3 4 5

Grow Again?

YES // NO

PLANT LOG

PLANT NAME

CROP TYPE

Plant Type	Sun Requirement	Water Requirement	Life Cycle
O Vegetable O Fruit O Herb O Ornamental			O Annual O Biennial O Perennial

SOWN FROM SEED

Supplier
Cost

Date Sown

Date Germinated
Date Planted Out

Date Harvested/Bloomed

STARTED TRANSPLANT

Supplier

Cost

Date Planted

Date Harvested/Bloomed

GROWING NOTES *(pests, fertilizers, disease, unexpected weather conditions, etc.)*

OUTCOME

Total Yield in Pounds	Rate It?	Grow Again?
		**YES // NO**

PLANT LOG

PLANT NAME

CROP TYPE

Plant Type
○ Vegetable
○ Fruit
○ Herb
○ Ornamental

Sun Requirement

Water Requirement

Life Cycle
○ Annual
○ Biennial
○ Perennial

SOWN FROM SEED

Supplier

Cost

Date Sown

Date Germinated

Date Planted Out

Date Harvested/Bloomed

STARTED TRANSPLANT

Supplier

Cost

Date Planted

Date Harvested/Bloomed

GROWING NOTES *(pests, fertilizers, disease, unexpected weather conditions, etc.)*

OUTCOME

Total Yield in Pounds

Rate It?

1 2 3 4 5

Grow Again?

YES // NO

🌿 PLANT LOG 🌿

PLANT NAME

CROP TYPE

Plant Type	Sun Requirement	Water Requirement	Life Cycle
O Vegetable O Fruit O Herb O Ornamental			O Annual O Biennial O Perennial

SOWN FROM SEED

Supplier | Cost

Date Sown

Date Germinated | Date Planted Out

Date Harvested/Bloomed

STARTED TRANSPLANT

Supplier

Cost

Date Planted

Date Harvested/Bloomed

GROWING NOTES *(pests, fertilizers, disease, unexpected weather conditions, etc.)*

OUTCOME

Total Yield in Pounds	Rate It?	Grow Again?
	 1 2 3 4 5	YES // NO

PLANT LOG

PLANT NAME

CROP TYPE

Plant Type	Sun Requirement	Water Requirement	Life Cycle
○ Vegetable ○ Fruit ○ Herb ○ Ornamental			○ Annual ○ Biennial ○ Perennial

SOWN FROM SEED

Supplier

Cost

Date Sown

Date Germinated

Date Planted Out

Date Harvested/Bloomed

STARTED TRANSPLANT

Supplier

Cost

Date Planted

Date Harvested/Bloomed

GROWING NOTES *(pests, fertilizers, disease, unexpected weather conditions, etc.)*

OUTCOME

Total Yield in Pounds

Rate It?

1 2 3 4 5

Grow Again?

YES // NO

PLANT LOG

PLANT NAME

CROP TYPE

Plant Type
O Vegetable
O Fruit
O Herb
O Ornamental

Sun Requirement

Water Requirement

Life Cycle
O Annual
O Biennial
O Perennial

SOWN FROM SEED

Supplier | Cost

Date Sown

Date Germinated | Date Planted Out

Date Harvested/Bloomed

STARTED TRANSPLANT

Supplier

Cost

Date Planted

Date Harvested/Bloomed

GROWING NOTES *(pests, fertilizers, disease, unexpected weather conditions, etc.)*

OUTCOME

Total Yield in Pounds | Rate It? | Grow Again?

1 2 3 4 5 | YES // NO

🌿 PLANT LOG 🌿

PLANT NAME

CROP TYPE

Plant Type	Sun Requirement	Water Requirement	Life Cycle
O Vegetable			O Annual
O Fruit			O Biennial
O Herb			O Perennial
O Ornamental			

SOWN FROM SEED

Supplier : Cost

....

Date Sown

....

Date Germinated :: Date Planted Out

....

Date Harvested/Bloomed

STARTED TRANSPLANT

Supplier

....

Cost

....

Date Planted

....

Date Harvested/Bloomed

GROWING NOTES *(pests, fertilizers, disease, unexpected weather conditions, etc.)*

OUTCOME

Total Yield in Pounds	Rate It?	Grow Again?
	(1) (2) (3) (4) (5)	**YES // NO**

🌿 PLANT LOG 🌿

PLANT NAME

CROP TYPE

Plant Type	Sun Requirement	Water Requirement	Life Cycle
O Vegetable			O Annual
O Fruit			O Biennial
O Herb			O Perennial
O Ornamental			

SOWN FROM SEED

Supplier　　　　Cost

Date Sown

Date Germinated　Date Planted Out

Date Harvested/Bloomed

STARTED TRANSPLANT

Supplier

Cost

Date Planted

Date Harvested/Bloomed

GROWING NOTES *(pests, fertilizers, disease, unexpected weather conditions, etc.)*

OUTCOME

Total Yield in Pounds　　Rate It?　　　　　Grow Again?

1　2　3　4　5　　YES // NO

PLANT LOG

PLANT NAME

CROP TYPE

Plant Type | Sun Requirement | Water Requirement | Life Cycle
○ Vegetable
○ Fruit
○ Herb
○ Ornamental

Life Cycle
○ Annual
○ Biennial
○ Perennial

SOWN FROM SEED

Supplier   Cost

Date Sown

Date Germinated   Date Planted Out

Date Harvested/Bloomed

STARTED TRANSPLANT

Supplier

Cost

Date Planted

Date Harvested/Bloomed

GROWING NOTES *(pests, fertilizers, disease, unexpected weather conditions, etc.)*

OUTCOME

Total Yield in Pounds | Rate It? | Grow Again?

(1) (2) (3) (4) (5)

YES // NO

PLANT LOG

PLANT NAME

CROP TYPE

Plant Type
- O Vegetable
- O Fruit
- O Herb
- O Ornamental

Sun Requirement

Water Requirement

Life Cycle
- O Annual
- O Biennial
- O Perennial

SOWN FROM SEED

Supplier

Cost

Date Sown

Date Germinated

Date Planted Out

Date Harvested/Bloomed

STARTED TRANSPLANT

Supplier

Cost

Date Planted

Date Harvested/Bloomed

GROWING NOTES *(pests, fertilizers, disease, unexpected weather conditions, etc.)*

OUTCOME

Total Yield in Pounds

Rate It?

1 2 3 4 5

Grow Again?

YES // NO

PLANT LOG

PLANT NAME

CROP TYPE

Plant Type	Sun Requirement	Water Requirement	Life Cycle
○ Vegetable			○ Annual
○ Fruit			○ Biennial
○ Herb			○ Perennial
○ Ornamental			

SOWN FROM SEED

Supplier

Cost

Date Sown

Date Germinated

Date Planted Out

Date Harvested/Bloomed

STARTED TRANSPLANT

Supplier

Cost

Date Planted

Date Harvested/Bloomed

GROWING NOTES *(pests, fertilizers, disease, unexpected weather conditions, etc.)*

OUTCOME

Total Yield in Pounds	Rate It?	Grow Again?
	1 2 3 4 5	YES // NO

PLANT LOG

PLANT NAME

CROP TYPE

Plant Type
O Vegetable
O Fruit
O Herb
O Ornamental

Sun Requirement

Water Requirement

Life Cycle
O Annual
O Biennial
O Perennial

SOWN FROM SEED

Supplier

Cost

Date Sown

Date Germinated

Date Planted Out

Date Harvested/Bloomed

STARTED TRANSPLANT

Supplier

Cost

Date Planted

Date Harvested/Bloomed

GROWING NOTES *(pests, fertilizers, disease, unexpected weather conditions, etc.)*

OUTCOME

Total Yield in Pounds

Rate It?
1 2 3 4 5

Grow Again?
YES // NO

 # PLANT LOG

PLANT NAME

CROP TYPE

Plant Type	Sun Requirement	Water Requirement	Life Cycle
O Vegetable O Fruit O Herb O Ornamental			O Annual O Biennial O Perennial

SOWN FROM SEED

Supplier .... Cost

Date Sown

Date Germinated ...... Date Planted Out

Date Harvested/Bloomed

STARTED TRANSPLANT

Supplier

Cost

Date Planted

Date Harvested/Bloomed

GROWING NOTES *(pests, fertilizers, disease, unexpected weather conditions, etc.)*

OUTCOME

Total Yield in Pounds	Rate It?	Grow Again?
	1 2 3 4 5	**YES // NO**

✿ PLANT LOG ✿

PLANT NAME

CROP TYPE

Plant Type	Sun Requirement	Water Requirement	Life Cycle
O Vegetable O Fruit O Herb O Ornamental		💧 💧 💧	O Annual O Biennial O Perennial

SOWN FROM SEED

Supplier

Cost

Date Sown

Date Germinated

Date Planted Out

Date Harvested/Bloomed

STARTED TRANSPLANT

Supplier

Cost

Date Planted

Date Harvested/Bloomed

GROWING NOTES *(pests, fertilizers, disease, unexpected weather conditions, etc.)*

OUTCOME

Total Yield in Pounds	Rate It?	Grow Again?
	 1 2 3 4 5	**YES // NO**

PLANT LOG

PLANT NAME

CROP TYPE

Plant Type	Sun Requirement	Water Requirement	Life Cycle
◯ Vegetable			◯ Annual
◯ Fruit			◯ Biennial
◯ Herb			◯ Perennial
◯ Ornamental			

SOWN FROM SEED

Supplier   Cost

Date Sown

Date Germinated   Date Planted Out

Date Harvested/Bloomed

STARTED TRANSPLANT

Supplier

Cost

Date Planted

Date Harvested/Bloomed

GROWING NOTES *(pests, fertilizers, disease, unexpected weather conditions, etc.)*

OUTCOME

Total Yield in Pounds   Rate It?   Grow Again?

1 2 3 4 5   **YES // NO**

 PLANT LOG

PLANT NAME

CROP TYPE

Plant Type	Sun Requirement	Water Requirement	Life Cycle
O Vegetable O Fruit O Herb O Ornamental			O Annual O Biennial O Perennial

SOWN FROM SEED

Supplier | Cost

Date Sown

Date Germinated | Date Planted Out

Date Harvested/Bloomed

STARTED TRANSPLANT

Supplier

Cost

Date Planted

Date Harvested/Bloomed

GROWING NOTES *(pests, fertilizers, disease, unexpected weather conditions, etc.)*

OUTCOME

Total Yield in Pounds | Rate It?  | Grow Again? **YES // NO**

PLANT LOG

CROP TYPE

Plant Type	Sun Requirement	Water Requirement	Life Cycle
○ Vegetable			○ Annual
○ Fruit			○ Biennial
○ Herb			○ Perennial
○ Ornamental			

SOWN FROM SEED

Supplier

Cost

Date Sown

Date Germinated

Date Planted Out

Date Harvested/Bloomed

STARTED TRANSPLANT

Supplier

Cost

Date Planted

Date Harvested/Bloomed

GROWING NOTES *(pests, fertilizers, disease, unexpected weather conditions, etc.)*

OUTCOME

Total Yield in Pounds	Rate It?	Grow Again?
	1 2 3 4 5	**YES // NO**

 # PLANT LOG

PLANT NAME

CROP TYPE

Plant Type	Sun Requirement	Water Requirement	Life Cycle
O Vegetable O Fruit O Herb O Ornamental			O Annual O Biennial O Perennial

SOWN FROM SEED

Supplier

Cost

Date Sown

Date Germinated

Date Planted Out

Date Harvested/Bloomed

STARTED TRANSPLANT

Supplier

Cost

Date Planted

Date Harvested/Bloomed

GROWING NOTES *(pests, fertilizers, disease, unexpected weather conditions, etc.)*

OUTCOME

Total Yield in Pounds

Rate It?

Grow Again?

YES // NO

PLANT LOG

PLANT NAME

CROP TYPE

Plant Type	Sun Requirement	Water Requirement	Life Cycle
O Vegetable O Fruit O Herb O Ornamental			O Annual O Biennial O Perennial

SOWN FROM SEED

Supplier

Cost

Date Sown

Date Germinated

Date Planted Out

Date Harvested/Bloomed

STARTED TRANSPLANT

Supplier

Cost

Date Planted

Date Harvested/Bloomed

GROWING NOTES *(pests, fertilizers, disease, unexpected weather conditions, etc.)*

OUTCOME

Total Yield in Pounds

Rate It?
1 2 3 4 5

Grow Again?
YES // NO

PLANT LOG

PLANT NAME

CROP TYPE

Plant Type	Sun Requirement	Water Requirement	Life Cycle
O Vegetable O Fruit O Herb O Ornamental			O Annual O Biennial O Perennial

SOWN FROM SEED

Supplier

Cost

Date Sown

Date Germinated

Date Planted Out

Date Harvested/Bloomed

STARTED TRANSPLANT

Supplier

Cost

Date Planted

Date Harvested/Bloomed

GROWING NOTES *(pests, fertilizers, disease, unexpected weather conditions, etc.)*

OUTCOME

Total Yield in Pounds

Rate It?

Grow Again?

YES // NO

PLANT LOG

> **PLANT NAME**

> **CROP TYPE**

Plant Type	Sun Requirement	Water Requirement	Life Cycle
○ Vegetable			○ Annual
○ Fruit			○ Biennial
○ Herb			○ Perennial
○ Ornamental			

SOWN FROM SEED

Supplier   Cost

Date Sown

Date Germinated   Date Planted Out

Date Harvested/Bloomed

STARTED TRANSPLANT

Supplier

Cost

Date Planted

Date Harvested/Bloomed

GROWING NOTES *(pests, fertilizers, disease, unexpected weather conditions, etc.)*

OUTCOME

Total Yield in Pounds   Rate It?   Grow Again?

1 2 3 4 5   **YES // NO**

🌿 PLANT LOG 🌿

PLANT NAME

CROP TYPE

Plant Type
O Vegetable
O Fruit
O Herb
O Ornamental

Sun Requirement

Water Requirement

Life Cycle
O Annual
O Biennial
O Perennial

SOWN FROM SEED

Supplier

Cost

Date Sown

Date Germinated

Date Planted Out

Date Harvested/Bloomed

STARTED TRANSPLANT

Supplier

Cost

Date Planted

Date Harvested/Bloomed

GROWING NOTES *(pests, fertilizers, disease, unexpected weather conditions, etc.)*

OUTCOME

Total Yield in Pounds

Rate It?

1 2 3 4 5

Grow Again?

YES // NO

PLANT LOG

PLANT NAME

CROP TYPE

Plant Type	Sun Requirement	Water Requirement	Life Cycle
○ Vegetable ○ Fruit ○ Herb ○ Ornamental			○ Annual ○ Biennial ○ Perennial

SOWN FROM SEED

Supplier   Cost

Date Sown

Date Germinated   Date Planted Out

Date Harvested/Bloomed

STARTED TRANSPLANT

Supplier

Cost

Date Planted

Date Harvested/Bloomed

GROWING NOTES *(pests, fertilizers, disease, unexpected weather conditions, etc.)*

OUTCOME

Total Yield in Pounds   Rate It?   Grow Again?

1 2 3 4 5   YES // NO

PLANT LOG

PLANT NAME

CROP TYPE

Plant Type	Sun Requirement	Water Requirement	Life Cycle
O Vegetable O Fruit O Herb O Ornamental			O Annual O Biennial O Perennial

SOWN FROM SEED

Supplier

Cost

Date Sown

Date Germinated

Date Planted Out

Date Harvested/Bloomed

STARTED TRANSPLANT

Supplier

Cost

Date Planted

Date Harvested/Bloomed

GROWING NOTES *(pests, fertilizers, disease, unexpected weather conditions, etc.)*

OUTCOME

Total Yield in Pounds

Rate It?

Grow Again?

YES // NO

PLANT LOG

PLANT NAME

CROP TYPE

Plant Type	Sun Requirement	Water Requirement	Life Cycle
O Vegetable O Fruit O Herb O Ornamental			O Annual O Biennial O Perennial

SOWN FROM SEED

Supplier

Cost

Date Sown

Date Germinated

Date Planted Out

Date Harvested/Bloomed

STARTED TRANSPLANT

Supplier

Cost

Date Planted

Date Harvested/Bloomed

GROWING NOTES *(pests, fertilizers, disease, unexpected weather conditions, etc.)*

OUTCOME

Total Yield in Pounds

Rate It?

1 2 3 4 5

Grow Again?

YES // NO

PLANT LOG

PLANT NAME

CROP TYPE

Plant Type
O Vegetable
O Fruit
O Herb
O Ornamental

Sun Requirement

Water Requirement

Life Cycle
O Annual
O Biennial
O Perennial

SOWN FROM SEED

Supplier

Cost

Date Sown

Date Germinated

Date Planted Out

Date Harvested/Bloomed

STARTED TRANSPLANT

Supplier

Cost

Date Planted

Date Harvested/Bloomed

GROWING NOTES (pests, fertilizers, disease, unexpected weather conditions, etc.)

OUTCOME

Total Yield in Pounds

Rate It?

1 2 3 4 5

Grow Again?

YES // NO

PLANT LOG

PLANT NAME

CROP TYPE

Plant Type	Sun Requirement	Water Requirement	Life Cycle
◯ Vegetable ◯ Fruit ◯ Herb ◯ Ornamental			○ Annual ○ Biennial ○ Perennial

SOWN FROM SEED

Supplier

Cost

Date Sown

Date Germinated

Date Planted Out

Date Harvested/Bloomed

STARTED TRANSPLANT

Supplier

Cost

Date Planted

Date Harvested/Bloomed

GROWING NOTES *(pests, fertilizers, disease, unexpected weather conditions, etc.)*

OUTCOME

Total Yield in Pounds

Rate It?

Grow Again?

YES // NO

PLANT LOG

PLANT NAME

CROP TYPE

Plant Type	Sun Requirement	Water Requirement	Life Cycle
O Vegetable O Fruit O Herb O Ornamental			O Annual O Biennial O Perennial

SOWN FROM SEED

Supplier

Cost

Date Sown

Date Germinated

Date Planted Out

Date Harvested/Bloomed

STARTED TRANSPLANT

Supplier

Cost

Date Planted

Date Harvested/Bloomed

GROWING NOTES *(pests, fertilizers, disease, unexpected weather conditions, etc.)*

OUTCOME

Total Yield in Pounds

Rate It?

Grow Again?

YES // NO

PLANT LOG

PLANT NAME

CROP TYPE

Plant Type	Sun Requirement	Water Requirement	Life Cycle
• Vegetable • Fruit • Herb • Ornamental			○ Annual ○ Biennial ○ Perennial

SOWN FROM SEED

Supplier

Cost

Date Sown

Date Germinated

Date Planted Out

Date Harvested/Bloomed

STARTED TRANSPLANT

Supplier

Cost

Date Planted

Date Harvested/Bloomed

GROWING NOTES *(pests, fertilizers, disease, unexpected weather conditions, etc.)*

OUTCOME

Total Yield in Pounds

Rate It?

1 2 3 4 5

Grow Again?

YES // NO

PLANT LOG

PLANT NAME

CROP TYPE

Plant Type	Sun Requirement	Water Requirement	Life Cycle
O Vegetable			O Annual
O Fruit			O Biennial
O Herb			O Perennial
O Ornamental			

SOWN FROM SEED

Supplier

Cost

Date Sown

Date Germinated

Date Planted Out

Date Harvested/Bloomed

STARTED TRANSPLANT

Supplier

Cost

Date Planted

Date Harvested/Bloomed

GROWING NOTES *(pests, fertilizers, disease, unexpected weather conditions, etc.)*

OUTCOME

Total Yield in Pounds

Rate It?

Grow Again?

YES // NO

PLANT LOG

PLANT NAME

CROP TYPE

Plant Type	Sun Requirement	Water Requirement	Life Cycle
O Vegetable O Fruit O Herb O Ornamental			O Annual O Biennial O Perennial

SOWN FROM SEED

Supplier

Cost

Date Sown

Date Germinated

Date Planted Out

Date Harvested/Bloomed

STARTED TRANSPLANT

Supplier

Cost

Date Planted

Date Harvested/Bloomed

GROWING NOTES *(pests, fertilizers, disease, unexpected weather conditions, etc.)*

OUTCOME

Total Yield in Pounds

Rate It?

Grow Again?

YES // NO

PLANT LOG

PLANT NAME

CROP TYPE

Plant Type	Sun Requirement	Water Requirement	Life Cycle
O Vegetable			O Annual
O Fruit			O Biennial
O Herb			O Perennial
O Ornamental			

SOWN FROM SEED

Supplier   Cost

Date Sown

Date Germinated   Date Planted Out

Date Harvested/Bloomed

STARTED TRANSPLANT

Supplier

Cost

Date Planted

Date Harvested/Bloomed

GROWING NOTES *(pests, fertilizers, disease, unexpected weather conditions, etc.)*

OUTCOME

Total Yield in Pounds   Rate It?   Grow Again?

YES // NO

PLANT LOG

PLANT NAME

CROP TYPE

Plant Type	Sun Requirement	Water Requirement	Life Cycle
○ Vegetable			○ Annual
○ Fruit			○ Biennial
○ Herb			○ Perennial
○ Ornamental			

SOWN FROM SEED

Supplier

Cost

Date Sown

Date Germinated

Date Planted Out

Date Harvested/Bloomed

STARTED TRANSPLANT

Supplier

Cost

Date Planted

Date Harvested/Bloomed

GROWING NOTES *(pests, fertilizers, disease, unexpected weather conditions, etc.)*

OUTCOME

Total Yield in Pounds

Rate It?

1 2 3 4 5

Grow Again?

YES // NO

PLANT LOG

PLANT NAME

CROP TYPE

Plant Type
O Vegetable
O Fruit
O Herb
O Ornamental

Sun Requirement

Water Requirement

Life Cycle
○ Annual
○ Biennial
○ Perennial

SOWN FROM SEED

Supplier | Cost

Date Sown

Date Germinated | Date Planted Out

Date Harvested/Bloomed

STARTED TRANSPLANT

Supplier

Cost

Date Planted

Date Harvested/Bloomed

GROWING NOTES *(pests, fertilizers, disease, unexpected weather conditions, etc.)*

OUTCOME

Total Yield in Pounds

Rate It?

Grow Again?
YES // NO

PLANT LOG

PLANT NAME

CROP TYPE

Plant Type	Sun Requirement	Water Requirement	Life Cycle
○ Vegetable			○ Annual
○ Fruit			○ Biennial
○ Herb			○ Perennial
○ Ornamental			

SOWN FROM SEED

Supplier

Cost

Date Sown

Date Germinated

Date Planted Out

Date Harvested/Bloomed

STARTED TRANSPLANT

Supplier

Cost

Date Planted

Date Harvested/Bloomed

GROWING NOTES *(pests, fertilizers, disease, unexpected weather conditions, etc.)*

OUTCOME

Total Yield in Pounds	Rate It?	Grow Again?
	1 2 3 4 5	**YES // NO**

PLANT LOG

PLANT NAME

CROP TYPE

Plant Type	Sun Requirement	Water Requirement	Life Cycle
O Vegetable O Fruit O Herb O Ornamental			O Annual O Biennial O Perennial

SOWN FROM SEED

Supplier | Cost

Date Sown

Date Germinated | Date Planted Out

Date Harvested/Bloomed

STARTED TRANSPLANT

Supplier

Cost

Date Planted

Date Harvested/Bloomed

GROWING NOTES *(pests, fertilizers, disease, unexpected weather conditions, etc.)*

OUTCOME

Total Yield in Pounds | Rate It? | Grow Again?

YES // NO

PLANT LOG

PLANT NAME

CROP TYPE

Plant Type	Sun Requirement	Water Requirement	Life Cycle
O Vegetable			O Annual
O Fruit			O Biennial
O Herb			O Perennial
O Ornamental			

SOWN FROM SEED

Supplier

Cost

Date Sown

Date Germinated

Date Planted Out

Date Harvested/Bloomed

STARTED TRANSPLANT

Supplier

Cost

Date Planted

Date Harvested/Bloomed

GROWING NOTES *(pests, fertilizers, disease, unexpected weather conditions, etc.)*

OUTCOME

Total Yield in Pounds	Rate It?	Grow Again?
	1 2 3 4 5	**YES // NO**

PLANT LOG

PLANT NAME

CROP TYPE

Plant Type	Sun Requirement	Water Requirement	Life Cycle
O Vegetable O Fruit O Herb O Ornamental			O Annual O Biennial O Perennial

SOWN FROM SEED

Supplier

Cost

Date Sown

Date Germinated

Date Planted Out

Date Harvested/Bloomed

STARTED TRANSPLANT

Supplier

Cost

Date Planted

Date Harvested/Bloomed

GROWING NOTES *(pests, fertilizers, disease, unexpected weather conditions, etc.)*

OUTCOME

Total Yield in Pounds

Rate It?

Grow Again?

YES // NO

PLANT LOG

PLANT NAME

CROP TYPE

Plant Type	Sun Requirement	Water Requirement	Life Cycle
◯ Vegetable ◯ Fruit ◯ Herb ◯ Ornamental			◯ Annual ◯ Biennial ◯ Perennial

SOWN FROM SEED

Supplier | Cost

Date Sown

Date Germinated | Date Planted Out

Date Harvested/Bloomed

STARTED TRANSPLANT

Supplier

Cost

Date Planted

Date Harvested/Bloomed

GROWING NOTES *(pests, fertilizers, disease, unexpected weather conditions, etc.)*

OUTCOME

Total Yield in Pounds | Rate It? | Grow Again?

YES // NO

PLANT LOG

PLANT NAME

CROP TYPE

Plant Type	Sun Requirement	Water Requirement	Life Cycle
O Vegetable O Fruit O Herb O Ornamental			O Annual O Biennial O Perennial

SOWN FROM SEED

Supplier

Cost

Date Sown

Date Germinated Date Planted Out

Date Harvested/Bloomed

STARTED TRANSPLANT

Supplier

Cost

Date Planted

Date Harvested/Bloomed

GROWING NOTES *(pests, fertilizers, disease, unexpected weather conditions, etc.)*

OUTCOME

Total Yield in Pounds

Rate It?

Grow Again?

YES // NO

PLANT LOG

PLANT NAME

CROP TYPE

Plant Type	Sun Requirement	Water Requirement	Life Cycle
• Vegetable • Fruit • Herb • Ornamental			○ Annual ○ Biennial ○ Perennial

SOWN FROM SEED

Supplier

Cost

Date Sown

Date Germinated

Date Planted Out

Date Harvested/Bloomed

STARTED TRANSPLANT

Supplier

Cost

Date Planted

Date Harvested/Bloomed

GROWING NOTES *(pests, fertilizers, disease, unexpected weather conditions, etc.)*

OUTCOME

Total Yield in Pounds	Rate It?	Grow Again?
	1 2 3 4 5	YES // NO

PLANT LOG

PLANT NAME

CROP TYPE

Plant Type	Sun Requirement	Water Requirement	Life Cycle
O Vegetable			O Annual
O Fruit			O Biennial
O Herb			O Perennial
O Ornamental			

SOWN FROM SEED

Supplier

Cost

Date Sown

Date Germinated

Date Planted Out

Date Harvested/Bloomed

STARTED TRANSPLANT

Supplier

Cost

Date Planted

Date Harvested/Bloomed

GROWING NOTES *(pests, fertilizers, disease, unexpected weather conditions, etc.)*

OUTCOME

Total Yield in Pounds

Rate It?

Grow Again?

YES // NO

PLANT LOG

PLANT NAME

CROP TYPE

Plant Type	Sun Requirement	Water Requirement	Life Cycle
O Vegetable			O Annual
O Fruit			O Biennial
O Herb			O Perennial
O Ornamental			

SOWN FROM SEED

Supplier | Cost

Date Sown

Date Germinated | Date Planted Out

Date Harvested/Bloomed

STARTED TRANSPLANT

Supplier

Cost

Date Planted

Date Harvested/Bloomed

GROWING NOTES *(pests, fertilizers, disease, unexpected weather conditions, etc.)*

OUTCOME

Total Yield in Pounds | Rate It? | Grow Again?

1 2 3 4 5

YES // NO

PLANT LOG

PLANT NAME

CROP TYPE

Plant Type	Sun Requirement	Water Requirement	Life Cycle
O Vegetable O Fruit O Herb O Ornamental			O Annual O Biennial O Perennial

SOWN FROM SEED

Supplier   Cost

Date Sown

Date Germinated   Date Planted Out

Date Harvested/Bloomed

STARTED TRANSPLANT

Supplier

Cost

Date Planted

Date Harvested/Bloomed

GROWING NOTES *(pests, fertilizers, disease, unexpected weather conditions, etc.)*

OUTCOME

Total Yield in Pounds	Rate It?	Grow Again?
		YES // NO

PLANT LOG

PLANT NAME

CROP TYPE

Plant Type | Sun Requirement | Water Requirement | Life Cycle

Plant Type
- ◯ Vegetable
- ◯ Fruit
- ◯ Herb
- ◯ Ornamental

Life Cycle
- ◯ Annual
- ◯ Biennial
- ◯ Perennial

SOWN FROM SEED

Supplier | Cost

Date Sown

Date Germinated | Date Planted Out

Date Harvested/Bloomed

STARTED TRANSPLANT

Supplier

Cost

Date Planted

Date Harvested/Bloomed

GROWING NOTES *(pests, fertilizers, disease, unexpected weather conditions, etc.)*

OUTCOME

Total Yield in Pounds | Rate It? | Grow Again?

1 2 3 4 5

YES // NO

PLANT LOG

PLANT NAME

CROP TYPE

Plant Type	Sun Requirement	Water Requirement	Life Cycle
O Vegetable O Fruit O Herb O Ornamental			O Annual O Biennial O Perennial

SOWN FROM SEED

Supplier

Cost

Date Sown

Date Germinated

Date Planted Out

Date Harvested/Bloomed

STARTED TRANSPLANT

Supplier

Cost

Date Planted

Date Harvested/Bloomed

GROWING NOTES *(pests, fertilizers, disease, unexpected weather conditions, etc.)*

OUTCOME

Total Yield in Pounds

Rate It?

Grow Again?

YES // NO

PLANT LOG

PLANT NAME

CROP TYPE

Plant Type	Sun Requirement	Water Requirement	Life Cycle
○ Vegetable			○ Annual
○ Fruit			○ Biennial
○ Herb			○ Perennial
○ Ornamental			

SOWN FROM SEED

Supplier

Cost

Date Sown

Date Germinated

Date Planted Out

Date Harvested/Bloomed

STARTED TRANSPLANT

Supplier

Cost

Date Planted

Date Harvested/Bloomed

GROWING NOTES *(pests, fertilizers, disease, unexpected weather conditions, etc.)*

OUTCOME

Total Yield in Pounds	Rate It?	Grow Again?
	1 2 3 4 5	**YES // NO**

PLANT LOG

PLANT NAME

CROP TYPE

Plant Type
- O Vegetable
- O Fruit
- O Herb
- O Ornamental

Sun Requirement

Water Requirement

Life Cycle
- O Annual
- O Biennial
- O Perennial

SOWN FROM SEED

Supplier

Cost

Date Sown

Date Germinated | Date Planted Out

Date Harvested/Bloomed

STARTED TRANSPLANT

Supplier

Cost

Date Planted

Date Harvested/Bloomed

GROWING NOTES *(pests, fertilizers, disease, unexpected weather conditions, etc.)*

OUTCOME

Total Yield in Pounds

Rate It?

1 2 3 4 5

Grow Again?

YES // NO

PLANT LOG

PLANT NAME

CROP TYPE

Plant Type	Sun Requirement	Water Requirement	Life Cycle
O Vegetable			O Annual
O Fruit			O Biennial
O Herb			O Perennial
O Ornamental			

SOWN FROM SEED

Supplier   Cost

Date Sown

Date Germinated   Date Planted Out

Date Harvested/Bloomed

STARTED TRANSPLANT

Supplier

Cost

Date Planted

Date Harvested/Bloomed

GROWING NOTES *(pests, fertilizers, disease, unexpected weather conditions, etc.)*

OUTCOME

Total Yield in Pounds	Rate It?	Grow Again?
		**YES // NO**

 # PLANT LOG

PLANT NAME

CROP TYPE

Plant Type	Sun Requirement	Water Requirement	Life Cycle
O Vegetable O Fruit O Herb O Ornamental			O Annual O Biennial O Perennial

SOWN FROM SEED

Supplier   Cost

Date Sown

Date Germinated   Date Planted Out

Date Harvested/Bloomed

STARTED TRANSPLANT

Supplier

Cost

Date Planted

Date Harvested/Bloomed

GROWING NOTES *(pests, fertilizers, disease, unexpected weather conditions, etc.)*

OUTCOME

Total Yield in Pounds	Rate It?	Grow Again?
		**YES // NO**

PLANT LOG

PLANT NAME

CROP TYPE

Plant Type	Sun Requirement	Water Requirement	Life Cycle
○ Vegetable ○ Fruit ○ Herb ○ Ornamental			○ Annual ○ Biennial ○ Perennial

SOWN FROM SEED

Supplier

Cost

Date Sown

Date Germinated   Date Planted Out

Date Harvested/Bloomed

STARTED TRANSPLANT

Supplier

Cost

Date Planted

Date Harvested/Bloomed

GROWING NOTES *(pests, fertilizers, disease, unexpected weather conditions, etc.)*

OUTCOME

Total Yield in Pounds	Rate It?	Grow Again?
	1 2 3 4 5	YES // NO

PLANT LOG

PLANT NAME

CROP TYPE

Plant Type	Sun Requirement	Water Requirement	Life Cycle
O Vegetable O Fruit O Herb O Ornamental			O Annual O Biennial O Perennial

SOWN FROM SEED

Supplier · Cost

Date Sown

Date Germinated · Date Planted Out

Date Harvested/Bloomed

STARTED TRANSPLANT

Supplier

Cost

Date Planted

Date Harvested/Bloomed

GROWING NOTES *(pests, fertilizers, disease, unexpected weather conditions, etc.)*

OUTCOME

Total Yield in Pounds · Rate It? · Grow Again?

 **YES // NO**

PLANT LOG

PLANT NAME

CROP TYPE

Plant Type	Sun Requirement	Water Requirement	Life Cycle
Vegetable			○ Annual
Fruit			○ Biennial
Herb			○ Perennial
Ornamental			

SOWN FROM SEED

Supplier

Cost

Date Sown

Date Germinated

Date Planted Out

Date Harvested/Bloomed

STARTED TRANSPLANT

Supplier

Cost

Date Planted

Date Harvested/Bloomed

GROWING NOTES *(pests, fertilizers, disease, unexpected weather conditions, etc.)*

OUTCOME

Total Yield in Pounds	Rate It?	Grow Again?
	1 2 3 4 5	YES // NO

PLANT LOG

PLANT NAME

CROP TYPE

Plant Type	Sun Requirement	Water Requirement	Life Cycle
O Vegetable O Fruit O Herb O Ornamental			O Annual O Biennial O Perennial

SOWN FROM SEED

Supplier

Cost

Date Sown

Date Germinated

Date Planted Out

Date Harvested/Bloomed

STARTED TRANSPLANT

Supplier

Cost

Date Planted

Date Harvested/Bloomed

GROWING NOTES *(pests, fertilizers, disease, unexpected weather conditions, etc.)*

OUTCOME

Total Yield in Pounds	Rate It?	Grow Again?
		YES // NO

PLANT LOG

PLANT NAME

CROP TYPE

Plant Type	Sun Requirement	Water Requirement	Life Cycle
O Vegetable O Fruit O Herb O Ornamental			○ Annual ○ Biennial ○ Perennial

SOWN FROM SEED

Supplier

Cost

Date Sown

Date Germinated

Date Planted Out

Date Harvested/Bloomed

STARTED TRANSPLANT

Supplier

Cost

Date Planted

Date Harvested/Bloomed

GROWING NOTES *(pests, fertilizers, disease, unexpected weather conditions, etc.)*

OUTCOME

Total Yield in Pounds	Rate It?	Grow Again?
	1 2 3 4 5	YES // NO

PLANT LOG

PLANT NAME

CROP TYPE

Plant Type
O Vegetable
O Fruit
O Herb
O Ornamental

Sun Requirement

Water Requirement

Life Cycle
O Annual
O Biennial
O Perennial

SOWN FROM SEED

Supplier

Cost

Date Sown

Date Germinated

Date Planted Out

Date Harvested/Bloomed

STARTED TRANSPLANT

Supplier

Cost

Date Planted

Date Harvested/Bloomed

GROWING NOTES (pests, fertilizers, disease, unexpected weather conditions, etc.)

OUTCOME

Total Yield in Pounds

Rate It?
1 2 3 4 5

Grow Again?
YES // NO

PLANT LOG

> **PLANT NAME**

> **CROP TYPE**

Plant Type	Sun Requirement	Water Requirement	Life Cycle
○ Vegetable			○ Annual
○ Fruit			○ Biennial
○ Herb			○ Perennial
○ Ornamental			

SOWN FROM SEED

Supplier   Cost

Date Sown

Date Germinated   Date Planted Out

Date Harvested/Bloomed

STARTED TRANSPLANT

Supplier

Cost

Date Planted

Date Harvested/Bloomed

GROWING NOTES *(pests, fertilizers, disease, unexpected weather conditions, etc.)*

OUTCOME

Total Yield in Pounds   Rate It?   Grow Again?

1 2 3 4 5   **YES // NO**

PLANT LOG

PLANT NAME

CROP TYPE

Plant Type	Sun Requirement	Water Requirement	Life Cycle
O Vegetable			O Annual
O Fruit			O Biennial
O Herb			O Perennial
O Ornamental			

SOWN FROM SEED

Supplier

Cost

Date Sown

Date Germinated | Date Planted Out

Date Harvested/Bloomed

STARTED TRANSPLANT

Supplier

Cost

Date Planted

Date Harvested/Bloomed

GROWING NOTES *(pests, fertilizers, disease, unexpected weather conditions, etc.)*

OUTCOME

Total Yield in Pounds

Rate It?

Grow Again?

YES // NO

PLANT LOG

PLANT NAME

CROP TYPE

Plant Type	Sun Requirement	Water Requirement	Life Cycle
○ Vegetable ○ Fruit ○ Herb ○ Ornamental			○ Annual ○ Biennial ○ Perennial

SOWN FROM SEED

Supplier

Cost

Date Sown

Date Germinated

Date Planted Out

Date Harvested/Bloomed

STARTED TRANSPLANT

Supplier

Cost

Date Planted

Date Harvested/Bloomed

GROWING NOTES *(pests, fertilizers, disease, unexpected weather conditions, etc.)*

OUTCOME

Total Yield in Pounds	Rate It?	Grow Again?
	① ② ③ ④ ⑤	YES // NO

PLANT LOG

PLANT NAME

CROP TYPE

Plant Type	Sun Requirement	Water Requirement	Life Cycle
O Vegetable O Fruit O Herb O Ornamental			O Annual O Biennial O Perennial

SOWN FROM SEED

Supplier

Cost

Date Sown

Date Germinated

Date Planted Out

Date Harvested/Bloomed

STARTED TRANSPLANT

Supplier

Cost

Date Planted

Date Harvested/Bloomed

GROWING NOTES *(pests, fertilizers, disease, unexpected weather conditions, etc.)*

OUTCOME

Total Yield in Pounds

Rate It?

Grow Again?

YES // NO

PLANT LOG

PLANT NAME

CROP TYPE

Plant Type	Sun Requirement	Water Requirement	Life Cycle
O Vegetable			O Annual
O Fruit			O Biennial
O Herb			O Perennial
O Ornamental			

SOWN FROM SEED

Supplier

Cost

Date Sown

Date Germinated

Date Planted Out

Date Harvested/Bloomed

STARTED TRANSPLANT

Supplier

Cost

Date Planted

Date Harvested/Bloomed

GROWING NOTES *(pests, fertilizers, disease, unexpected weather conditions, etc.)*

OUTCOME

Total Yield in Pounds

Rate It?

1 2 3 4 5

Grow Again?

YES // NO

PLANT LOG

PLANT NAME

CROP TYPE

Plant Type	Sun Requirement	Water Requirement	Life Cycle
O Vegetable			O Annual
O Fruit			O Biennial
O Herb			O Perennial
O Ornamental			

SOWN FROM SEED

Supplier

Cost

Date Sown

Date Germinated

Date Planted Out

Date Harvested/Bloomed

STARTED TRANSPLANT

Supplier

Cost

Date Planted

Date Harvested/Bloomed

GROWING NOTES *(pests, fertilizers, disease, unexpected weather conditions, etc.)*

OUTCOME

Total Yield in Pounds

Rate It?

Grow Again?

YES // NO

PLANT LOG

PLANT NAME

CROP TYPE

Plant Type	Sun Requirement	Water Requirement	Life Cycle
◯ Vegetable			◯ Annual
◯ Fruit			◯ Biennial
◯ Herb			◯ Perennial
◯ Ornamental			

SOWN FROM SEED

Supplier

Cost

Date Sown

Date Germinated

Date Planted Out

Date Harvested/Bloomed

STARTED TRANSPLANT

Supplier

Cost

Date Planted

Date Harvested/Bloomed

GROWING NOTES *(pests, fertilizers, disease, unexpected weather conditions, etc.)*

OUTCOME

Total Yield in Pounds	Rate It?	Grow Again?
	1 2 3 4 5	YES // NO

 # PLANT LOG

PLANT NAME

CROP TYPE

Plant Type	Sun Requirement	Water Requirement	Life Cycle
O Vegetable O Fruit O Herb O Ornamental			O Annual O Biennial O Perennial

SOWN FROM SEED

Supplier | Cost

Date Sown

Date Germinated | Date Planted Out

Date Harvested/Bloomed

STARTED TRANSPLANT

Supplier

Cost

Date Planted

Date Harvested/Bloomed

GROWING NOTES *(pests, fertilizers, disease, unexpected weather conditions, etc.)*

OUTCOME

Total Yield in Pounds | Rate It?  | Grow Again? **YES // NO**

PLANT LOG

PLANT NAME

CROP TYPE

Plant Type	Sun Requirement	Water Requirement	Life Cycle
Vegetable			○ Annual
Fruit			○ Biennial
Herb			○ Perennial
Ornamental			

SOWN FROM SEED

Supplier

Cost

Date Sown

Date Germinated

Date Planted Out

Date Harvested/Bloomed

STARTED TRANSPLANT

Supplier

Cost

Date Planted

Date Harvested/Bloomed

GROWING NOTES *(pests, fertilizers, disease, unexpected weather conditions, etc.)*

OUTCOME

Total Yield in Pounds

Rate It?

1 2 3 4 5

Grow Again?

YES // NO

❧ PLANT LOG ❧

PLANT NAME

CROP TYPE

Plant Type	Sun Requirement	Water Requirement	Life Cycle
O Vegetable O Fruit O Herb O Ornamental			○ Annual ○ Biennial ○ Perennial

SOWN FROM SEED

Supplier

Cost

Date Sown

Date Germinated

Date Planted Out

Date Harvested/Bloomed

STARTED TRANSPLANT

Supplier

Cost

Date Planted

Date Harvested/Bloomed

GROWING NOTES *(pests, fertilizers, disease, unexpected weather conditions, etc.)*

OUTCOME

Total Yield in Pounds

Rate It?

Grow Again?

YES // NO

~ PLANT LOG ~

PLANT NAME

CROP TYPE

Plant Type	Sun Requirement	Water Requirement	Life Cycle
O Vegetable			O Annual
O Fruit			O Biennial
O Herb			O Perennial
O Ornamental			

SOWN FROM SEED

Supplier

Cost

Date Sown

Date Germinated

Date Planted Out

Date Harvested/Bloomed

STARTED TRANSPLANT

Supplier

Cost

Date Planted

Date Harvested/Bloomed

GROWING NOTES *(pests, fertilizers, disease, unexpected weather conditions, etc.)*

OUTCOME

Total Yield in Pounds	Rate It?	Grow Again?
		**YES // NO**

PLANT LOG

PLANT NAME

CROP TYPE

Plant Type	Sun Requirement	Water Requirement	Life Cycle
O Vegetable O Fruit O Herb O Ornamental			○ Annual ○ Biennial ○ Perennial

SOWN FROM SEED

Supplier

Cost

Date Sown

Date Germinated

Date Planted Out

Date Harvested/Bloomed

STARTED TRANSPLANT

Supplier

Cost

Date Planted

Date Harvested/Bloomed

GROWING NOTES *(pests, fertilizers, disease, unexpected weather conditions, etc.)*

OUTCOME

Total Yield in Pounds

Rate It?

Grow Again?

YES // NO

PLANT LOG

PLANT NAME

CROP TYPE

Plant Type	Sun Requirement	Water Requirement	Life Cycle
○ Vegetable			○ Annual
○ Fruit			○ Biennial
○ Herb			○ Perennial
○ Ornamental			

SOWN FROM SEED

Supplier

Cost

Date Sown

Date Germinated · Date Planted Out

Date Harvested/Bloomed

STARTED TRANSPLANT

Supplier

Cost

Date Planted

Date Harvested/Bloomed

GROWING NOTES *(pests, fertilizers, disease, unexpected weather conditions, etc.)*

OUTCOME

Total Yield in Pounds	Rate It?	Grow Again?
		**YES // NO**

PLANT LOG

PLANT NAME

CROP TYPE

Plant Type	Sun Requirement	Water Requirement	Life Cycle
O Vegetable			O Annual
O Fruit			O Biennial
O Herb			O Perennial
O Ornamental			

SOWN FROM SEED

Supplier

Cost

Date Sown

Date Germinated

Date Planted Out

Date Harvested/Bloomed

STARTED TRANSPLANT

Supplier

Cost

Date Planted

Date Harvested/Bloomed

GROWING NOTES *(pests, fertilizers, disease, unexpected weather conditions, etc.)*

OUTCOME

Total Yield in Pounds

Rate It?

Grow Again?

YES // NO

PLANT LOG

PLANT NAME

CROP TYPE

Plant Type	Sun Requirement	Water Requirement	Life Cycle
Vegetable			○ Annual
Fruit			○ Biennial
Herb			○ Perennial
Ornamental			

SOWN FROM SEED

Supplier

Cost

Date Sown

Date Germinated

Date Planted Out

Date Harvested/Bloomed

STARTED TRANSPLANT

Supplier

Cost

Date Planted

Date Harvested/Bloomed

GROWING NOTES *(pests, fertilizers, disease, unexpected weather conditions, etc.)*

OUTCOME

Total Yield in Pounds	Rate It?	Grow Again?
		**YES // NO**

PLANT LOG

PLANT NAME

CROP TYPE

Plant Type	Sun Requirement	Water Requirement	Life Cycle
O Vegetable O Fruit O Herb O Ornamental			○ Annual ○ Biennial ○ Perennial

SOWN FROM SEED

Supplier

Cost

Date Sown

Date Germinated   Date Planted Out

Date Harvested/Bloomed

STARTED TRANSPLANT

Supplier

Cost

Date Planted

Date Harvested/Bloomed

GROWING NOTES *(pests, fertilizers, disease, unexpected weather conditions, etc.)*

OUTCOME

Total Yield in Pounds

Rate It?

Grow Again?

YES // NO

PLANT LOG

PLANT NAME

CROP TYPE

Plant Type	Sun Requirement	Water Requirement	Life Cycle
O Vegetable O Fruit O Herb O Ornamental			O Annual O Biennial O Perennial

SOWN FROM SEED

Supplier

Cost

Date Sown

Date Germinated

Date Planted Out

Date Harvested/Bloomed

STARTED TRANSPLANT

Supplier

Cost

Date Planted

Date Harvested/Bloomed

GROWING NOTES *(pests, fertilizers, disease, unexpected weather conditions, etc.)*

OUTCOME

Total Yield in Pounds

Rate It?

1 2 3 4 5

Grow Again?

YES // NO

PLANT LOG

PLANT NAME

CROP TYPE

Plant Type
O Vegetable
O Fruit
O Herb
O Ornamental

Sun Requirement

Water Requirement

Life Cycle
O Annual
O Biennial
O Perennial

SOWN FROM SEED

Supplier

Cost

Date Sown

Date Germinated

Date Planted Out

Date Harvested/Bloomed

STARTED TRANSPLANT

Supplier

Cost

Date Planted

Date Harvested/Bloomed

GROWING NOTES *(pests, fertilizers, disease, unexpected weather conditions, etc.)*

OUTCOME

Total Yield in Pounds

Rate It?

1 2 3 4 5

Grow Again?

YES // NO

PLANT LOG

CROP TYPE

Plant Type	Sun Requirement	Water Requirement	Life Cycle
Vegetable			○ Annual
Fruit			○ Biennial
Herb			○ Perennial
Ornamental			

SOWN FROM SEED

Supplier

Cost

Date Sown

Date Germinated

Date Planted Out

Date Harvested/Bloomed

STARTED TRANSPLANT

Supplier

Cost

Date Planted

Date Harvested/Bloomed

GROWING NOTES *(pests, fertilizers, disease, unexpected weather conditions, etc.)*

OUTCOME

Total Yield in Pounds

Rate It?

1 2 3 4 5

Grow Again?

YES // NO

SPECIAL BONUS!

Thank you for purchasing our journal! To show our appreciation, we thought we'd send you a gift in the form of a **free mini E-book**!

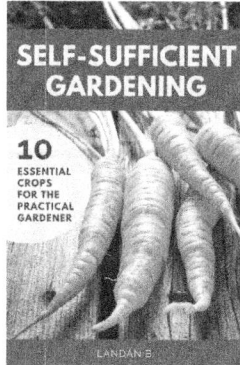

We think you'll enjoy SELF-SUFFICIENT GARDENING, 10 Essential Crops for the Practical Gardener.

On top of receiving this PDF download, you'll get to enjoy insider access to all of our future publications for FREE!

Scan the code below with your smartphone camera to claim your gift:

https://bit.ly/3fhPT4q

Printed in Great Britain
by Amazon